call me

Laia Sales Merino

Flirtation #36

ò

salò press

This collection copyright © 2025 by Laia Sales Merino

All rights reserved. No part of this publication may be reproduced, stored in a retrieval system, rebound or transmitted in any form or by any means, electronic, mechanical, photocopying, recording or otherwise, without the prior written permission of the author and publisher. This book is sold subject to the condition that it shall not by way of trade or otherwise be lent, resold, hired out or otherwise circulated without the publisher's prior consent in any form of binding or cover other than that in which it is published.

Some of these poems appeared previously in the following journals: *Sal en la herida* in *MMPP*; *led blue* in *harana poetry*

978-1-917264-07-5

Printed and Bound by 4Edge

Cover design and layout by Salò Press
Art by edurne marco garcía

Typeset by Sophie Essex

Published by:
Salò Press
85 Gertrude Road
Norwich
UK

editorsalòpress@gmail.com
www.salòpress.com

To my sisters, Sara i Gina (the loves of la meva vida), and to Mercè, who always called me

Contents

londres butterflies	2
Lung infection	3
ya me llamas	6
Adéu	8
day i forget how to speak English	9
Sal en la herida	11
night paseos	12
noodle soup	13
led blue	15
videocall	16
subtitles.pret.mireia.3	17
what's your favourite reggaeton song?	20
t'estimo	21
call me	23

Hola?

londres butterflies

ayyy no sé   maybe
i heard a woman in august
speaking spanish on the phone
tendía su ropa roja
a conjunto con su voz abierta
in her tooting garden   i felt many
mariposas   so i said to Tess   SÍ
i'll move with you

to LONDON
now in this night bus
i have a cold   an appetite for drama
i text you que "me muero </3"
there are too many places we're tied with
we try to untie from

and i sneeze   some butterflies
they stick   to the bus floor
i stare at them   with red ojos
amor meu   a bus ride away
many many lights
a suitcase
an address in streatham

Lung infection
for Tess

I'm very ill so I've been waiting
since midday on this bed
contemplating the room.
For example, the bookcase.
Fell on top of me this morning.
Didn't hurt me
much
but it broke.
Now I have books
on the floor, the windowsill,
around me on this
¾ bed,
inside the wardrobe,
under this
¾ bed, on my thighs.
I'm waiting.
My lungs hurt a lot.
The mould on the walls,
sneaky black,
shaggy white,
is staring at me.
Fuck.
I place pillows behind my shoulders
to breathe
but I can't.
I decide to get up,
knock on your door.
You call 111.
The nurse says *call an ambulance*
and *good luck*.

I think she thinks I'll die.
We call an uber.
At A&E we wait.
The loo sign makes me laugh.
I show you.
We laugh a lot.
My laugh sounds like asphyxiation
and it bothers the people
in the waiting room
but I can't stop.
Help.

Hola mama! Com estàs?

ya me llamas
for Brayan

dj, who the fuck are you
playing, coño!
then i see you, corazón, about
to leave, no, bésame o
y me pierdo del
todo

>*salud!* wait,
>*hablas español?* we
>stare no blinking
>at each other, throats
>ablaze with tequila
>like a caress, *bésame*
>*o…*

o me muero
we stumble into a corner
shop, get crisps, kiss
at the till whisper like
*en mi casa tengo…*call
a cab, SÍ

>in the morning, last night's
>bésame-o-me-pierdo-in
>this-puta-ciudad
>sound hungoverly
>when we lick each
>*fuck*

you say you going
to the barber's in brixton
i say i'm late picking
mi amiga up from…
liverpool station, creo

                        ya me llamas

                                  ¿sí
                        mi amor?

Adéu
for Deshawn

We were hungry.
A woman says *señorita,*
tiene la bolsa en el piso.
You say *I've never*
seen a woman leave
her purse on the floor

You say *I feel like we're*
in a movie, someone
brings us tequila

If you could
go back in time,
would you do it? At my place
we dim the lights

I should kiss you ahora

we stay still until

my breath on your collarbone

we fuck as if you had

booked your flight

already

to Milwaukee

(home)

At night I dream again
that you're leaving without
saying goodbye

day i forget how to speak English

last time i swallowed
the morning-after pill was
two days after he raped
me   a night that i've been
trying to untie from
the last thirteen years   i'm scared
that my body will remember
the pill and again   i'll see
him   this time in London
everywhere   so i text you
my love   say i'll do
the emergency IUD instead
but now in this NHS room DO YOU UNDERSTAND ENGLISH?
HAVE YOU HAD UNPROTECTED SEX? WHEN? HOW MANY SEXUAL PARTNERS? WHEN WAS YOUR LAST PERIOD?
HOW CAN YOU NOT KNOW? DO YOU NOT KEEP TRACK?
DO YOU UNDERSTAND, LAYLA?
the doctor and the nurse
give me a glass of water
and a pill
se'm queden mirant
fins que me l'empasso.

Ay, diga-li hola a l'abuela!

Sal en la herida
for Cisco

Why you speaking spanish when you can speak perfect english?
We stare at the bouncer,
cuchillos bright behind our ojos.
You kicking us out cause we speaking spanish to each other?
We needed to dance more and ese
puto imbécil de mierda
has forbidden entry to our lenguas.
El hijueputa del bouncer fuck all of them.
Miro a la luna spitting upon us.
Cisco yo me voy pa streatham pa la casa then.
When I get off the bus I see
a bar y otro bar y otro bar.
I place a couple phrases on my lips,
take out my ID like I don't
have to go to work mañana
to sell books and smile at everybody.
Text you que I got home alright.
Tres tequilas please.
I swallow pedacitos of myself
so that bailo hacia ese man y ese man,
let them know
que I want salt on my tongue,
I want salt, que quiero sal
en mi lengua
ahora.

night paseos

                        my body
            lit living-rooms   la luna   blink
    of streetlight   your eyes into mine   black cats
        en mis ojos   every flicker of a lighter
my eyes get used   to the nightsky   till i can swallow all
            of its cries   its clammy face   hasta llenarme
                and won't need
                                    dinner

noodle soup
> *for Nat*

speaking in catalan
is making me
tipsy   i struggle with
the chopsticks
getting broth inside
my eyes *tia, i mira*
que la Julie em va ensenyar
        remember when we drank
        glen's at glasgow's flat parties?
i've stopped writing
poems   i've started
rolling tobacco rolling
corazones rolling
malsons watching
netflix when i'm home
        remember when we texted
        bon dia and bona nit every day and night?
at least there's music
at brixton station
 i have five noodles
 hanging down my boca
 i meet eyes with
 a man in a suit
 i wink at him

¡HOLA, ABUELA!
¿CÓMO ESTÁS? ¿QUIÉN ESTÁ GANANDO?

led blue
for Leo

este poema retumbando en mi cabeza when
we breathe fast up the stairs
mis ojos en tu nuca   chained nape
and the promise of your lips en mi piel SÍ
tv like another kind of luna   we
por fin and your body blessed
i hope you know that you are blessed
que your homeland's in your eyes
bebé we fuck by the lights
of some movie you choose
you ask me what i like   y de repente
i'm fucking him   not you   till you
say something in my language
boca llena de tu sound   my london
chico brazilian coração
your lips like a cruz heavy
like a cruz
i want all of you all of you—

videocall

i want to tell you que i spent the morning waiting for the sun que yesterday i fainted on the tube and a woman helped me que today i got a bus to the centre and my friend said she couldn't come so i watched a dance crew on the street and went back home with the same bus que lately i walk down la calle with three cuts between my eyebrows que i can't pay rent this month que i have malsons again que instead of breakfast i smoke que i'm seeing him everywhere que i think the bed is the best invention ever made que last saturday i forgot que

subtitles.pret.mireia.3
for Mireia & V & all my friends

Pues tia la setmana passada,
Deshawn left his flat in Norwich early morning.

Me quedé solita en su cama,
tried to fall back hard into a dream.

Lloré al lado de su radiador apagado,
my arms wrapped around it like mala hierba.

[inaudible: 03:22:04]
how my ribs shook.

Sequé el agua leakeando de su nevera with a red cloth.
I ran my fingertips above his mirror,

stared at myself. Una pestanya sobre la galta.
Fuck.

"Buen vuelo bonic."
He left.

Volví a su cama. En una esquina me abrazé las costillas,
blew a promise to myself. It caught fire.

Entonces llamé a V.
I closed his door and walked to her house.

Ella me besó,
baked a mollete for me in the oven.

Ese mollete con mantequilla
made me forget about the hot night sky of his eyes.

Acariciaba las mantas del sofá de V
until her sofa became a boat.

Y pues tia… Això.
But how are you, bonica?

Pues mira, mama, que aquí a Londres…
Que em passo la vida al transport
i gairebé no em puc pagar l'habitació
i us trobo molt a faltar…

what's your favourite reggaeton song?
for Anto

1. red roses see-through top stuck to my skin redrawing tattoos bra useless ojos deshilándose quiero perrear till my eyeliner melts completely y mi cara rebrille and i lose one eye lense *she your friend? sí, she* te miro solita en un rincón lips cidersparkling your hips leaving me voicemails every beat making your spine hurt pero tú sigues bailando *él tenía kind eyes, che... anto, pero ¿te duele mucho la espalda? i'm sorry for drinking tequila instead of dancing with you,* pero

2. stumble out the club with tangled ojos y la luna leakeando and will she kiss you and will she lick your spine and hold it forever ojalá i see your hands writing verdades y me enredo en ellas fumo observando la calle que no es nuestra esta and what will we eat chips or their *señoritaswhereyougoin* pero se nos ha quitado el hambre, pero

3. in the bus we breaking grammars construyendo teléfonos / *anto quiero dormir acurrucada en el huequito de tu collarbone*
       no,   *o,*   *y*

t'estimo
> *for Adam*

You're here on my last day,
your ojos still cloudless cielos.
I miss our flat in Maryhill.
We used to tremble with dreams
of so much home.
Sometimes I google Glasgow,
stare at the images for hours
until the blue of
the night sky there,
the *shite fuck fucking fuck*
conversations, until the donuts
at the deli where Sabrina worked,
until your lips.
Gina says time spent in transport allows
the heart to catch up with the journey.
I'm still in that plane
from Glasgow to London,
never caught up, me perdí.
Your hair still noche encendida.
Most of my suitcases
packed already.

I, bueno, que he estat pensant que...
Bueno, això,

call me

call me because i decided all this in one night in a hotel room my landlord paid for, room 333
callme ecause i'm in a taxi with my mother sisters father to stansted airport, no return
callame cause i just found your piece of paper arrugado in my pocket, 10 numbers
cállame cuse too many dripping images susurrándose in my mind, corazón
callaame ue everywhere dejé many many love cartas
callamame que i'm closing my english now abriendo mi boca
allamame rque three canciones se persiguen locas y estriadas por mi piel
llamame prque siento muchísimas mariposas vivas y verdes y ahora y el aeropuerto ya
llámame porque londres ha sido sábanas brillantes miradas enormes llamadas de vueltas ayyy

que torno.

Laia Sales Merino is a poet from the Catalan Pyrenees currently based in Barcelona. She speaks and writes across three languages: Catalan, Spanish and English. Her work can be found in *Ambit, Asymptote, e-Radical, GASHER, harana poetry* and *Variant Literature*, among others, and has been included in several anthologies such as *SMEOP: Urban* from Black Sunflowers, *I'll Show You Mine* (UEA Publishing Project) and *Letters from Nowhere / Ocho historias de viaje* (John & Vida White Endowment Fund). She holds an MA in Poetry from the University of East Anglia.